Know Yourself Like Your Success Depends on It

Michal Stawicki

"See yourself in the mirror of your mind to find yourself."

— **Debasish Mridha**

CONTENTS

1   Realization Begins Your Journey   1

2   Philosophy Is the Key to Change   5

3   An Unheralded Weapon: Self-talk   9

4   Tracking Is the Rudder That Keeps You on Course   13

5   Journaling Opens Your Mind   19

6   Self-Analysis is Simple   25

7   Meditation Illuminates Your Purpose   29

8   Prayer Puts Things in Perspective   33

9   Your Mission   39

10   In Summary   41

11   Look in the Mirror and Start Now   45

     Bonus: Free Resources   49

     About the Author   55

1. REALIZATION BEGINS YOUR JOURNEY

"You can, you should, and if you're brave enough to start, you will."—
Stephen King

Stephen King is referring to writing. Everyone has a story to tell, and in this age of digital publishing, anyone can tell one. But only a few tell their story, even if it's become ridiculously easy to do so. Only those courageous enough to show themselves will do it.

I have quite a few friends who are self-published authors. I learn from them. I realized one of the qualities that differentiate doers from talkers while reading a friend's wonderful book *Journey Within My Heart*. She knew herself. She was able to tell the story from within her heart because she knew what was hidden there.

My enlightenment didn't stop there. In the first quarter of 2013, I participated in an online Transformational Contest organized by *Early to Rise*. Part of that participation involved contributing to an online forum. I enjoyed being part of a lively community that supported and cheered each other on. It was the most positive bunch of people I've ever met. But most who joined did not turn that positive energy into any lasting success.

I followed those who continued the projects they began: they wrote books, they started businesses, they launched blogs. Those individuals had a deep insight into their own souls.

Finally, I realized the broader picture: success is directly dependent on your ability to examine yourself.

This realization brought me to the idea of this series. If this ability to look within is common among the doers, are there other such characteristics? Can they be learned? Can they catapult an individual to success?

Yes, yes, and yes.

Success requires more than good self-analysis, just as being a great basketball player requires much more than great free-throw shooting ability.

But it's certainly handy. And if a player also develops superb efficiency in 2-point and 3-point throws and is above average at reading the game, predicting opponents' moves, and playing well in a team, suddenly synergy develops. Now he is recognized as a great player.

Self-analysis is the skill that has been mastered by countless successful people throughout history.

Marcus Aurelius, Roman emperor in the second century, was the most powerful man on the planet in his time. He is famous today due to *Meditations*, a journal he kept while waging war in the defense of the Empire. These notes reveal insights into his heart and show the self-discipline he attained through self-analysis.

Jim Rohn was a self-made millionaire. He struggled to keep afloat and manage his debts for the first six years of his career. Then he met his mentor, Earl Shoaff, and become a millionaire over the next six. He was a great preacher and practitioner of self-knowledge. He recommended writing and keeping a journal, and did so for over fifty years, from the age of 25.

Napoleon Bonaparte climbed to the role of French Emperor from modest means. He built a powerful country out of the ashes of revolution within sixteen years. Under his rule, France defeated multiple armies across Europe. He still made time to write his memoirs while doing so.

Many saints kept journals. Often their journals are the only written works they left behind.

Self-analysis is not limited to discoveries you make through journaling. Saints almost unanimously practiced reflection and spiritual exercises during yearly retreats. Saint Mother Teresa of Calcutta didn't leave many written works, but her confessors and spiritual directors kept her notes from retreats.

All those I've mentioned have left lasting marks in history. The nature of their achievements is secondary. Some of them just wanted to go to Heaven, some of them wanted to build successful businesses and add value to the world, some wanted to serve their countries to the maximum of their capabilities, and some just wanted to rule the world. But they all had in common the habit of examining, assessing, and correcting themselves.

Their methods varied. Some preferred meditation, some journaling, others spiritual exercises or some other activity. This ability to examine yourself is so commonly seen among successful people that no one pursuing success can ignore the importance of this foundation. It is one of the cornerstones of success.

If you don't have experience in this area, it is not a serious obstacle. Self-analysis is a skill. As such, it can be developed. I can help you. For sixteen years, I avoided self-analysis at all costs. I was more than a bit frustrated about my situation—a long commute, a job without prospects of promotion, a lukewarm spiritual life—but I was covering this frustration by spending my time reading fiction and playing computer games. I preferred to anesthetize myself rather than pull myself together and seriously examine what was bothering me and how to change it.

Eventually though, I did change. And if I—with the attitude I once had—could change, you can do it too.

When I started to analyze myself on a regular basis, results in my life materialized. I passed a few professional exams and earned a couple of specialized certificates for my day job. I started writing and publishing, and my books actually sold. I bought the house my wife had been dreaming about for years. I lost 15% of my body weight and my fitness performance is now better than it was in my teenage years.

My attention to self-analysis isn't the sole reason I gained these successes. Self-analysis is only one element in a set of success-building factors. But it's a necessary one.

Self-analysis may even become the cornerstone of your success, however you define it. As the examples above demonstrate, the use of this is not restricted to politics or business. Deeper insight into yourself can help you with anything.

Remember:

- Success directly depends on your ability to examine yourself.
- Self-analysis is a skill and as such can be developed.
- The use of self-analysis is not restricted to politics or business. Deeper insight into yourself can help you with anything.

2. PHILOSOPHY IS THE KEY TO CHANGE

Let's talk a little about philosophy, a branch of knowledge begun by Socrates.

The word *philosophy* derives from Greek *philosophia*, which means "love of knowledge, pursuit of wisdom; systematic investigation." In today's materialistic world, that may seem meaningless. Nevertheless, reflect on how many man-hours have been spent studying philosophy through the centuries; "millions" is not an exaggeration.

Today, most of us consider intangible subjects (like philosophy) irrelevant, not worth studying. In a fast-paced, solution-focused world, philosophy offers no how-to tips. An easy verdict follows: philosophy is obsolete.

I don't believe so, as this "obsolete idea," the pursuit of wisdom, has been the source of many modern concepts. Playing it down is like playing down blacksmithing. Who needs those metalworker's skills nowadays? Only hobbyists. But basic blacksmithing techniques developed over centuries are the foundation of the modern metallurgy industry, without which we wouldn't have even electrical cords.

Intangible leads to tangible. Socrates' follower, Aristotle, is credited with setting the foundation for all modern science. The device you read this book on was invented as an indirect result of Socrates' love for wisdom. Your lifestyle is possible because this man did something differently than his compatriots several thousand years ago.

Why is it relevant? Because Socrates' life motto was, "Know thyself."

This is how far self-knowledge can lead you.

Socrates wasn't a picture of success, as we understand it today. He spent his life thinking and talking. He had no job. He went to the local market every day to meet people and talk with them. His wife scolded him often and didn't understand his drive for wisdom at all. Each time Socrates went to the market, he hoped that one of his friends would invite him for a dinner so he could fill his empty stomach and avoid his wife at the same time.

His lifestyle didn't win him many supporters. The authorities didn't like him spreading his ideas among the young. He was a revolutionist from the start and he finished as one. He was charged with corrupting the youngsters and sentenced to death. He was poisoned but continued to talk with his students and ask them questions to his last breath.

Socrates could have avoided condemnation if he'd recanted his teachings. Socrates could have just said he was wrong, that he caused unnecessary tribulation, and he would have been left alone. Instead, he chose death.

Not the brightest thing to do, is it?

But Socrates knew himself. He knew that life without the ability to pursue wisdom in his own way would be meaningless. He had sacrificed decades to the study of wisdom, and he didn't intend to recant his principles to satisfy a bunch of oligarchs.

This act of accepting death rather than a change of course was the crowning achievement of his life. Socrates was happy to die. Wisdom was all he cared for, and he defended it until his death.

I said it in the introduction to this series: success is not wealth or one-time achievement; it is process and small disciplines. By this definition, Socrates was a smashing success.

Knowing yourself is neither a guarantee of worldly success nor great health. Self-knowledge is not a guarantee you'll achieve anything. However, it is a prerequisite for *everything* that you'd consider worthwhile. It's the foundation on which you can build.

Take a look at the five most common regrets among dying people. They are all about living according to your values. I guess "regretting nothing at the moment of death" may be an alternative definition of success.

Of course, studying yourself won't just lead to a righteous life. Inner peace is perhaps the ultimate result of such study, but there are other, useful effects. Steve Jobs, Jim Rohn, and Marcus Aurelius were not hermits who sat reflecting in caves. Yet much of their success may be credited to the knowledge they gained through self-analysis.

You may gain similar advantages, both spiritual and tangible.

Why? Because you are your greatest asset. Your success depends wholly on you. You can face obstacles, but armed with your internal resourcefulness you can overcome them. You may get lucky, but if you screw things up it won't do you any good. Your attitude and reactions determine your actions and the results you get.

Self-analysis is a way to learn about your greatest asset and then to put this knowledge into action.

If you don't know yourself, you can waste vast amounts of resources. "Overnight" rock stars who later hit rock bottom and broken lottery winners are both vivid examples of such a fate. If you know yourself, you can transform your obstacles into stepping-stones.

Success is all about personal change. Once you decide to change something, your inputs are how achievements are materialized. While a person is miserable and considers herself a failure, success is unlikely. To achieve success, you must first *become* success. You need to transform from underachiever into overachiever. Then the results you want will happen.

In order to change, you need to know what and how to change. You must know your starting position. Self-analysis provides just that. Only through knowing yourself can you conclude what you need to change in yourself and the most likely methodology to achieve it.

First and foremost, the result of self-analysis is a *positive* self-awareness. You may be overly self-aware, as in the case of shy people, who are so focused on their every word and gesture that they cannot utter a word in the presence of an attractive person of the opposite sex. However, solid and constant practice of self-analysis brings the positive kind of awareness.

"The power within us makes us into the image of that to which we give our attention." — Wallace D. Wattles

The constant practice of analyzing yourself in the right way shifts your focus from secondary things to what's important in your life. Suddenly you discover many activities, habits, and situations that don't serve you well. You may not have been aware of them prior to examining the inside of your heart. What's even more important, you'll discover the activities and situations that bring you fulfillment and happiness. You'll start developing new good habits to get more of that.

Your life is busy and complex. Your resources and capabilities are always limited. Awareness provides much needed simplicity. Once you know yourself, your strengths and weaknesses, you'll know where more time and effort is needed, and where less is required.

The direct fruit of self-awareness is focus. For example, I'm a "willpower machine." I can start any given new habit just like that, out of the blue. I don't need preparation or upfront consideration. I have more than thirty daily habits. Most of them I do every day without a stumble. My friends have nicknamed me Mr. Consistency. But I discovered that whenever I start a new habit, lapses in my old habits are unavoidable. In the week when I started practicing Tiny Habits, I broke a more than half-year-long streak in my gratitude journaling and on another day an over thirty-day-long streak in meditation. This knowledge caused me to not pursue new habits on a whim anymore.

Time plus effort equals results. The more you invest in those two factors, the more rapidly you will get results. While there is always a possibility of burnout when you overdo your pursuit of success, self-analysis protects you even from that. When you know yourself, you also know your limits.

So get to know yourself. Become aware of your vices and virtues. Get clarity. Ignore the nonessential in your life and focus on the substantial.

Analysis ->Awareness ->Focus ->Results

Remember:

- Self-knowledge is a prerequisite for *everything* that you'd consider worthwhile. It's the foundation on which you can build.
- In order to change, you need to know what and how to change.
- The direct fruit of self-awareness is focus; the constant practice of analyzing yourself in the right way shifts your focus from secondary things to what's important in your life.
- Analysis ->Awareness ->Focus ->Results

3. AN UNHERALDED WEAPON: SELF-TALK

Are you familiar with *Psycho-Cybernetics* by plastic surgeon Maxwell Maltz? In this groundbreaking book, he demonstrates how self-image dictates everything in a person's life. If you reflect, you will find this to be true. We are actually unable to do things that contradict any "I'm the person, who ..." thoughts we may have.

If you know deep inside your heart that you are not the type to cheat on your spouse, you won't. It is as simple as that. Why then, is cheating so common? Unfortunately, all too many people have a 'backdoor' to their opinion about this, which gives them an out:

"I would never cheat on my spouse, WHEN I'm sober";
"I would never cheat on my wife, IF she was fair to me";
"I would never cheat on my husband IF it was some poor, ugly guy."

Those *"I'm the person, who..."* sentences are at the core of your being. According to Maltz, those statements determine all your actions. Actually, I think the key factor determining your actions is your personal philosophy, but we both agree that the impetus to act comes from within. Your internal world determines your actions in the external world.

For me, the most intriguing part of *Psycho-Cybernetics* is Maltz's discussions about hypnosis. Under the influence of a hypnotizer, people start to believe different things about themselves. It can empower or disempower them. An athlete may be convinced that his arm is so heavy that he is unable to raise it from the table. A shrinking violet may be convinced that he is attractive and has no problem talking to women. Consequently, he is able to flirt with a gal from the audience right away.

The whole difference is in what those hypnotized people perceive as truth about themselves. It's not just the wish of the author or a mind-catching theory. In his plastic surgery practice, Maltz observed the relationship between people and the "truth" they carried.

He had patients who turned their lives around after plastic surgery. When their physical defects were fixed, they immediately fixed their relationships or careers. But he also had patients who looked at the mirror after the surgery and told themselves there was no difference, although it was clearly visible to anyone besides them.

Those poor patients' self-image painted a false version of themselves that was stronger than reality. Their senses reported a change, yet their internal interpreting mechanism filtered out this data. They couldn't see it, and they couldn't turn their lives around.

Maltz recommended using visualization on a regular basis to improve your self-image. I prescribe self-analysis. My imagination has withered over the years, unfortunately, so I could not usefully apply his advice. I found it difficult imagining a new future. Could someone who has lain in a bed for sixteen years get up and run? I cannot sit for even five minutes and visualize myself behaving differently. At any rate, I'm unable to do it on regular basis; it's an excruciating effort for me.

But I discovered that I can adjust my self-image with constant self-analysis practices. That's much easier for me than visualizing images in my head. I can sit down for ten minutes every day with a pen and notepad and note the flow of my self-talk. I can fire questions at myself, and when I do, I'm aware when my answers don't reflect reality.

The relation between self-image and success is simple. It's the starting point of all your actions. You can't achieve results if you are so blinded by your self-perception that you are not able to start an action in the direction you need to go. If you do nothing, you'll achieve nothing.

I've dreamed about being a writer since early childhood. As soon as I learned to read, I put myself in the stories I read and changed them in my mind. That was my favorite leisure activity. But in my mind, I was not a person who *wrote* stories.

I didn't think I had the potential to be a writer, so I didn't write. The facts were against my convictions: my academic writing was praised, and I wrote a lot on forums about my hobbies, and people were engaging with my stories there. But in my mind, I didn't have what it took to be a writer. I finally took a step towards becoming a writer at the age of 33, when I developed my personal mission statement.

The power of self-image is enormous. I had years of mental inertia to overcome. Even after I wrote in my mission statement the sentence *I'm becoming a writer*, I started very timidly. I wrote my first article a month after that! It took another couple of months for me to begin work on a short story. It took me six months to start my first book and almost a year before I started to write every day.

I was the same person I am today, with more or less the same set of skills and command of language. I could have started immediately. I would have published about five more books by now if I had. But my internal resistance was too great.

When I was researching self-talk for my book about overcoming shyness, I was amazed to discover that many top performers, especially in sports, focus on self-talk more than on techniques or skills. At the highest level of professional sports they consider skills and techniques a given. You can't reach that level without them. What allows them to beat their opponents is not more time spent honing their skills, but more focus on perfecting their internal dialog.

Sportsmen and their coaches are paid for results. They've discovered that in sports the right self-talk generates results. So they ignore the debate about whether self-talk and self-image are "proper disciplines" because results are the only measure that counts.

I encourage you to adopt the same attitude. Your self-talk IS important. It DOES determine your self-image. And your self-image DOES dictate your actions. You talk to yourself more than any other person in the world. In your head, a constant chatter takes place. And if you're like many other people, your self-talk isn't encouraging you.

Self-analysis will help you to know yourself better, to target negative issues in your mind and untangle them. Once they are solved, your potential will be unlocked.

Intangible leads to tangible. Several months ago I changed the sentence in my personal mission statement to *I'm a writer*. I track all my writing activities and you should know this: Since I changed that statement, my word count has increased by 38%. It works.

Remember:

- You are unable to do things that contradict any "*I'm the person, who...*" thoughts you may have.
- Self-image is the starting point of all your actions.
- Your self-talk determines your self-image and your self-image dictates your actions.

4. TRACKING IS THE RUDDER
THAT KEEPS YOU ON COURSE

The easiest way to become aware about the performance of anything is to track it. To progress in any given area, simply begin to track the essential metrics. You don't have to decide that you'll be mindful about it. Once you start tracking, you'll put your attention into it, and it will happen automatically. Focus and results are just natural aftereffects.

Towards the end of my weight loss quest, I decided to keep a food journal. I was just six pounds away from my dream weight, but I hadn't progressed an ounce during the previous month. Once I started to note down every scrap of food and every gulp of drink that contained calories, I got an immediate awareness of my calorie intake. Mind you, I didn't intend to track calories, I just wanted to track my consumption. Nonetheless, the decision to do it freshened my focus. I didn't consciously change my diet. I didn't change my exercise routine. Yet eight weeks later, I reached my target of 138 lbs.

An additional advantage of tracking is the realization you get when you see accurate data. All too often, we create an incorrect reality in our minds and take action on it; this doesn't lead to the results we want. However, the act of gathering and analyzing real-life data blows away our illusions. As the Bible says: "You shall know the truth and the truth shall set you free."

In September 2013, I started to track my writing. I was convinced that I write much faster in Polish than in English. A couple of months into this activity, I checked my average word count for writing in both languages. To my amazement the difference was tiny, less than one word per minute. Thanks to this feedback, I overcame another obstacle in my career as an author.

I consider tracking an effective tool in sharpening my awareness. It's not as effective as, let's say, half an hour of meditation, but it provides results that I can use to make meaningful changes. Today's society loves instant gratification and regards all kinds of intangible practices as suspicious. Tracking is as down-to-earth as you can get. You measure, write down, and analyze.

So ... if you want an improvement technique that will deliver immediately tangible results—unlike activities such as prayer, meditation, or visualization—tracking is an ideal start. It's the perfect beginning, which can lead you to more advanced (and less tangible) techniques.

Pick anything you want to progress at. Anything. Time management, weight loss, a professional skill needed at your job, social relationships, spirituality, fitness performance ...

It really doesn't matter what you choose. There is a useful metric in any activity. Even in a mystical area like spirituality there is bound to be something you can track. I'm a Christian and I decided to better my spiritual life. I set myself a goal of a ten-minute-long Bible study every day. It's a very simple and tangible metric. It's done or it's not done. I don't try to count angels on a pinhead or estimate how often I think evil thoughts.

So pick whatever you want and attach some metric to this activity. I assure you that your focus and awareness will naturally increase in that area.

The next step is to make tracking as easy as possible. Your goals shouldn't be overly ambitious in the first place. Don't try to exercise in the gym for three hours every day if all you've done up to now is a walk to the bus stop, and you don't really have three hours to allocate without drastically cutting your attention from other things. And the tracking of a discipline must be easier than the discipline itself. It's pointless to start hard and fast just to recognize after a month that you abandoned tracking your small discipline because it overly burdened your schedule or mind. My suggestion is to start slowly and gradually. Expand your tracking activities in both scope and detail according to your progress.

Don't try some elaborate process to track your new habit. If tracking habits is to seamlessly fit into your day, the actions have to come naturally to you. For example, if you are a tech geek and your mobile is an integral part of you, find some appropriate app for this purpose. If you are old-school, use pen and paper. With just a small sheet of paper, you can track anything. I can't imagine a recording system simpler than pen and paper. You do something and immediately write it down. You can also use tools that track your activities in the background, such as Fitbit, which registers in the cloud the number of steps you took or the length and quality of your sleep. Of course, to track like that, you do have to keep the gadget with you all the time. It certainly beats counting your steps in your head.

I spend half my life in front of my computer, so I track many activities using computer files. I love the convenience and how easy it is to analyze the data. But the other half of my life I'm away from my computer, so I use a pocket notepad to jot down the metrics I track (like expenses) and I enter them into a digital file later.

With the pen in my hand, I used to track my food intake, how I spent my day, and my ten-minute habits. By using both digital recording and paper recording, I could track activities wherever I was, without needing 24/7 digital access.

Whatever you decide to use, it should be appropriate to your discipline and convenient to use. For example, if you want to track how much time you spend on social media, I think using the RescueTime app, which gathers this data unobtrusively in the background, is a more sensible strategy than manually writing down your login and logout times.

Just don't overdo the automation. The point of tracking is to increase your awareness and focus. When you note down your information manually, it leaves a trace in your memory and awareness. But if tracking data is automatically harvested, there is the danger you'll forget to check it and will gain no benefit.

You should examine your tracking data in detail from time to time anyway, but with automatic systems; it's a necessity to plan to do this.

It's impossible to track your habits consistently and not make progress.

It is true that some will say, *"I tracked calories, but it didn't help me."* But they don't add, *"So I soon abandoned the tracking."*

For most metrics, you won't get any meaningful information from only a few days tracking. Track some metrics for a year and then claim it doesn't work.

As my experience with the food journal shows, when you start tracking a given activity, results appear "on their own." When you start thinking about metrics, your mind expands and considers a wide field of inputs, some subconsciously. Your awareness increases without your visible effort. Your attention translates into results, utilizing your focus.

That's the foremost effect of tracking. It serves as the lens of your focus. It is almost as effective as constant conscious effort but needs much lower energy input on your part.

Tracking is not all benefits; there are downsides.

The biggest one is self-criticism. Tracking reveals the truth and it can be painful. When you don't pay attention to your deeds or performance, it's easy to lie to yourself.

"Oh, it's just a single donut, it won't make any difference. Besides, I'm not even overweight." However, when you observe a "single donut" appearing every other day, it's much harder to keep a straight face.

Your brain uses smoke and mirrors to keep you on your current course. It doesn't like changes and the easiest way to maintain the status quo is to come up with lies and excuses. As long as you don't try to see through the smoke and mirrors, this strategy works perfectly well.

All too often, when we start to track something, we discover that our true deeds, attitude, and performance are not as nice as we thought they were. And we become disappointed with ourselves.

At this moment, unnecessary self-criticism or even self-loathing may start. Beware of them. They can lead you farther astray. Think about it. What do you usually do when you are disappointed by your performance? You beat yourself up and then console yourself with a quick boost of dopamine—whether it is gained through some sugar, fat, or quick mindless win (like reaching the eighth level in a game in twelve minutes, which allows you to feel you've accomplished something). None of these activities bring you closer to the results you desire. What is more, they are cementing your destructive behaviors.

It's another mind trick that will keep you dormant.

Remember: tracking is not a club to beat yourself with. It's a feedback loop. Yes, it will reveal some unpleasant facts. What else would you expect? Why are you tracking in the first place? To improve, of course. And if you are not perfect yet, it's only natural to encounter performance that you'll want to improve.

Don't think badly about yourself. Think badly about your wrongdoing. And, regardless of the data in your feedback loop, don't get offended by the figures, or the tracking system. Continue tracking, it's a foolproof method for improvement. It surely beats doing nothing or surrendering to your vices. If you stop tracking you may feel better, but you won't BE better.

Remember:

- You can track anything; to progress in any given area, begin to track the essential metrics.
- Two main benefits of tracking are increased awareness and accurate data.
- Be aware of tracking downsides: disappointment and self-criticism.
- It's impossible to track your habits consistently and not make progress.

Action Items:

- Pick the area in which you want to progress.
- Brainstorm a few metrics that can be applicable in a given area; attach at least one metric to this activity. (I recommend pen and paper for this activity.)
- Choose your tracking method; make it as easy as possible and integrate it with your lifestyle and current habits.
- Don't overdo the automation; examine your tracking data in detail regularly.
- Use tracking as a feedback loop; draw conclusions and use them to improve your tracking methods and performance.

5. JOURNALING OPENS YOUR MIND

Journaling seems to be the most common method of self-analysis among successful people. This may be because for centuries it was the only practical way of analyzing oneself, at least in Western culture. Our ancestors had no access to the wide variety of gadgets and software we now enjoy. However, quill pens and ink were accessible to most who were educated sufficiently to be literate.

The extent of journaling also produced ample evidence of its effectiveness. Successful people used this tool so often that it's easy to point it out as a common activity among them.

So, what kind of journals can help you look deeper into your soul? Any kind of documentation you make about your thoughts, emotions, and actions could be considered a journal. And any time you note these things, the mere process will help you to know yourself in a more intimate way.

You might document your reflections about a single project, recording the obstacles and solutions attached to it.

You may daily jot your thoughts on loose sheets of paper. Even if you lose them, the sheer act of noting them down will have left some mark on your consciousness (in the same way I described while explaining tracking).

You can write down your goals, break them down into weekly and daily actions, and monitor your progress.

You can write about your emotions or track your moods.

You can focus on a single topic, almost as if you were simply tracking your goal, but besides the dry data, you could add additional notes on how you feel, why you failed, and how you plan to reach your next milestone.

Craig Ballantyne, the Canadian millionaire, writes small daily achievements in his journal.

The journaling of Janet Conner, the author of *Writing Down Your Soul*, can be best described as "freestyle journaling." Every day, she furiously writes down everything that comes to her mind. She bombards her conscious mind with question and listens to the answers from within.

My favorite kind of journal is a gratitude journal. Keeping such a diary forces you to look for positives. Gratitude journals are widely popular among achievers, and recent research indicates that this simple activity can keep you happy.

It certainly can shield you from desperation. One of my friends on Coach.me lost her boyfriend in a car accident. When it happened, she had been registering her thoughts in a gratitude journal for more than a year and a half. Sabrina kept journaling about the things she was grateful for, although it sometimes felt surreal to her. Nonetheless, she stuck with her discipline and she has been able to function more or less normally. Her "gratitude streak" is 900+ days long. Gratitude journaling wasn't a magic cure for her grief, but it certainly helped her to keep her sanity and integrity at that terrible time.

As you see, there are plenty of journaling activities you can pick from. And there is no right way. You should journal the way you feel helps your life path.

There are not only different types of journals, there are also different media in which to record your entries. You are no longer restricted by an old definition of a journal: *"A book in which you write down your personal experiences and thoughts."* Today's definition is more like "a record of experiences, ideas, or reflections kept regularly for private use." Pen and paper are still favorites for many, but you can also record your entries using software, in different types of digital files, in audio or video, online or offline.

Naturally, you are not restricted to a single system. I keep a few traditional journals, and I track my habits on the Coach.me application, my writing in an Excel file, and my business activities in a text file. I share the last one on my online Progress Journal.

I recommend handwriting; it is powerful, as it activates your motor memory. But maybe you are one of the generation who has never written more than 500 words at a time. Then stay with typing, or record short audio remarks on your mobile. The way you decide to keep your journal should depend on your lifestyle and preferences.

This book is not about journaling *per se*. There are a multitude of volumes written about how to start and maintain the habit of journaling. If you decide to seek detailed instructions on what and how, just search. You'll find countless books.

However, I'll give you a quick overview.

To help you design an appropriate journaling habit, go through these four steps:

Step 1. Don't overwhelm yourself.

If you are a novice at journaling, don't start too ambitiously. Nowadays, I am a journaling machine, but I started from a single entry about my wife in a gratitude journal. For over three months, it was the only journaling activity I performed daily. With hindsight, I see it was the perfect way to develop a journaling habit via the Tiny Habits method. I love my wife dearly, so it was not difficult at all. In fact, I looked forward each day for the moment I noted down some nice thing about her.

On the other hand, I suggest you do as much as you can. The more data you "input," and the more commitment you make, the faster you will see results out of this discipline. Currently, I spend about half an hour a day on journaling. This level of commitment gives me a deep insight into my heart. I was in awe when I read that Wally Amos wrote his personal mission statement during a single flight to Hawaii. But less than a month ago, I defined my single motivating purpose in less than five minutes. The more you practice self-analysis, the faster you will be able to extract high-quality answers about yourself.

Step 2. Start the journal you want to sustain.

We are talking here about developing a long-term journaling habit. You may do some tracking from time to time—I did that with my time tracking—or till you accomplish the goal you set. I did this with my diet log, abandoning it about a week after reaching my dream weight. But journaling is a different kind of animal altogether.

The value from journaling comes principally over time. The more you do it, the more you'll get from it. Thus, you should start in a way you'll want to continue.

Nothing is certain but death and taxes … and your journaling habit should have third place in that sentence. You may of course abandon the journaling habit one day, but any thought of that should be as far from your mind as thoughts about your death.

Step 3. You should like it.

As I'm suggesting you continue a journaling habit long term, you have to enjoy the process. It's a must when you begin journaling. It can't be yet another chore on your to-do list. You don't need more of them, do you?

That's why I recommend starting with some kind of gratitude journal. It may be an achievements journal, where you note what you did right, or just which tasks you've finished that day. It may be a journal about someone else. For example, I have a gratitude journal in which I note at least three things about each of my kids for which I'm grateful.

You might keep a standard gratitude journal in which you simply note for what and whom are you grateful. I've noticed on Coach.me that people very often add why they are grateful for a particular thing, event, or person. Doing this will hook you right into the source of your gratitude.

You don't have to like journaling, but liking any new habit will help you maintain it. My most time consuming habit is writing 1,000 words a day six times a week and at least 400 words on Sundays. Trust me—I don't always enjoy writing my 1,000 words. Sometimes it's more of a chore than a pleasure, but I can maintain it. See Step 2.

Step 4. Review your journal regularly.

You should review your journal from time to time. Just recording your experiences and reflections will increase your self-knowledge and self-awareness. However, reading and reflecting on your notes will speed up this process manyfold.

Keep in mind that you will be reviewing your entries when you decide how to keep your journal. Don't make your entries too big. For example, if you decide on a video journal, you'll need almost the same amount of time to watch your entries as you spend recording them. You may not have the time for this. I write much more slowly than I read, so I can afford to write for twenty to thirty minutes a day and still review the entries once a week. If you decide on an audio journal, you'll have many opportunities to listen to your thoughts: while commuting, walking, driving, etc.

Remember:

- Journaling is the most common method of self-analysis among successful people.
- There are all kinds of journals both in the subject matter and technique of journaling.
- Handwriting activates your motor memory.

Action Items:

- Start small.
- Aim for sustainability; pick the method suitable for your lifestyle that will be easy for review.
- Make your journaling enjoyable; pick fascinating subject matter for the start (for me it was a gratitude diary about my wife).
- Journal regularly, preferably on a daily basis.
- Review your journal regularly; set a schedule and stick with it.

6. SELF-ANALYSIS IS SIMPLE

When I was creating my personal mission statement in autumn 2012, I realized the mechanism my brain had been using to keep me dormant. I'd been avoiding self-analysis; if I ever sacrificed a minute to reflect on myself, my mind quickly provided the rationale to cease: *"You are a sucker and you can't change it."* Case closed.

I functioned like that for at least sixteen years. Those years were not exactly wasted, but I could have done much more if I'd paid attention to what was happening inside me. Heck! What is the use of an advanced mind if it's not properly employed?

The creation of a personal mission statement requires a lot of self-analysis. Within a month, I did more of this than I'd done in my whole life. And realizing how important self-analysis was to my well-being, I jotted down a sentence in my mission statement: *"Knowing myself is the most powerful thing I can do and in the end the sole weapon I possess."*

Continual repetition of this sentence (together with my entire mission statement) impacted my subconscious sufficiently that I built a self-analysis habit within seven months.

The forming of this habit was not conscious at all. I was absorbing a lot of personal development material at that time, which included many self-analysis exercises like goal setting and examining strengths. I knew I wanted to transform myself, to become an entrepreneur, but I had no idea how to go about it. Defining my idea required more questions and answers. I started to work on my personal development and it involved a lot of tracking. I started a few journals.

All these activities together built my self-analysis processes into the habit I now have. Now, I'll reverse engineer this for you, so can prepare yourself to start a similarly useful habit.

I keep my self-analysis sessions short: from ten to twenty minutes. Yes, I follow my own Ten-Minute Philosophy. It's a chunk of time long enough to return significant advantages (if you maintain the activity regularly), yet short enough not to crowd a schedule.

When I began this discipline, I didn't set aside a special time for it.

I would stuff it in any available time window, such as in the morning before a commute, or at the office before starting work. Sometimes I'd take a break during work, and sometimes I'd do it late in the evening when the kids were asleep.

After a couple of months, I decided this self-analysis was so important to me that I made it a part of my morning routine. Since then, I've been doing it before my commute to work. To block this time, I started waking up fifteen minutes earlier (for example, today it was 3:30 a.m. instead of 3:45 a.m.).

Each morning, I sit with pen in my hand and jot down my reflections in a journal. As you see, I don't need any fancy tools to perform my self-analysis session. As I handwrite my ruminations, I restrict the session's time to ten to twenty minutes. I only use about half a page. If the subject is more complex and requires more time and space, I stop, and I continue the next day.

The starting point of my session is usually a question.
Why did I behave in such and such way yesterday?
What does the success of my latest book mean to me?
What can I do daily to strengthen relationships with my kids?
I write the question as a headline and answer it comprehensively.

Sometimes I also employ my imagination, especially when referring to the future:
What would my perfect day look like?
What do I want my life to look like in ten years?
With questions like those, I not only write down the answers, but visualize them first.

I'm a solopreneur: my business depends on my decisions and actions alone. Quite often, I use my self-analysis sessions to examine my business actions and plans:
How can I get and keep subscribers?
What do I have to do to plan the next book launch?
These imagination exercises and business ideas often come from what I read or listen to: blog posts, books, podcasts, etc.

I complete these self-analysis sessions on a schedule, six days a week. It's important to me, so I don't allow myself to do it randomly when I feel like it. On Sundays, I read the week's six journal entries.

You can set your own frequency when designing your self-analysis process. However, I strongly advise to make it regular, preferably every day.

If you decide on a weekly session, then do it once a week. Just keep in mind that any habit you only do once a week will take a long time to effect meaningful change.

Doing things daily multiplies a weekly effort by much more than seven times. Doing things daily creates momentum, and the effect is much stronger than the amount of energy and focus you can put into a single instance of your activity.

It's my opinion, based on my experience, that paying attention to self-analysis **every day** will facilitate you mastering it not seven but seventy times faster. You'll get better results more quickly.

Whether you self-analyze five times a day, or weekly, biweekly or monthly, a focus on self-analysis will boost all parts of your life. Do it at a pace you can maintain, for consistency is more important than anything else. Just do it.

The result of self-journaling is deeper self-knowledge. It is useful in absolutely everything. You'll get gains in purposefulness, resoluteness, single-mindedness, strength of will, strength of character, firmness, intentness, and decision-making.

You'll definitely start saving a ton of time when making decisions. I remember being contacted at the beginning of April 2014 by a man from Germany who offered to translate my book. I experienced a surge of anxiety. What guarantee did I have that he wouldn't steal my work? What guarantee did I have that he would do his job well?

If you don't know yourself well, such anxiety is the ideal feed for procrastination. Every time you are about to do something about a problem at hand, apprehension like this will fill your mind. In the end, you'll do nothing. The only way to get rid of these doubts is to take action.

Thanks to my self-analysis sessions, I immediately recognized and targeted these anxious thoughts. Then I ridiculed them and sent the manuscript to the guy. What did I have to lose? Publishing rights in a market I wasn't going to publish in anytime soon? That was the worst-case scenario. And as usual, my fears didn't materialize. My new partner in Germany, Christian, has turned out to be a very reliable fellow. I've received several payments from him, from 1.7%

to 4% of my "day job" salary. That's quite a tangible output from the intangible power of self-analysis, isn't it? I need just 25 to 60 such deals and I could quit my job.

Decisiveness is hard to estimate, but it is absolutely huge in terms of saved time and energy (instead of wasting these precious resources through doubting and second-guessing yourself).

Thanks to the level of self-insight I've developed, I've been able to make similar decisions in a heartbeat, multiple times. When Chris Bell volunteered to edit my book *Master Your Time* and help me market it, I didn't hesitate a second. The worst he could have done was steal my book. Well, I could always write another one. But he didn't, and *Master Your Time* was my first professionally edited book. It was also the first to become a best seller.

An example of this decisiveness is my contract with Archangel Ink. I was contacted by them just a couple of weeks after finalizing the purchase of my house. I had spent every single dime I had, except for the last 1,000 euros from my book royalties. When the publisher requested a $1,500 initial deposit, my internal warning mechanism went immediately on overload. I didn't have $1,500 to spare! But my consciousness also immediately recognized the opportunity. That was my chance and I knew it.

The rest is history. I signed the contract and my sales increased, my royalties doubled, and the number of my readers expanded.

I'm firmly convinced that self-analysis provides you concrete and measurable advantages.

Remember:

- Your brain avoids self-analysis to keep you dormant.
- You don't need any fancy tools to perform self-analysis sessions.
- The basic self-analysis tools are insightful questions.
- Doing things daily multiplies your effort.
- The results of self-knowledge are purposefulness, resoluteness, single-mindedness, strength of will, strength of character, firmness, intentness, and decision-making.

7. MEDITATION ILLUMINATES YOUR PURPOSE

Tony Stubblebine, a CEO and cofounder of Coach.me, is a big advocate of meditation. No wonder, really. While meditation might not look like much to the outside observer, those who have used it—including scientists—confirm that it significantly boosts productivity, reduces stress, improves creativity, and increases focus and memory.

How can it do this?

Coach.me explains it in this article:

http://blog.coach.me/habit-of-the-day-why-meditation-increases-your/

You'll also find links to university research about the benefits of meditation.

The simple act of sitting still and breathing for a few minutes boosts productivity! Isn't that a wondrous discovery for our society filled up with materialism?

The number one obstacle to starting meditation is your attitude. Most people don't even consider doing meditation because they think it's some semi-magical activity below their dignity. Pat Flynn, an online entrepreneur, described this kind of attitude very aptly in one of his podcasts:

"Meditation was always something that was really weird to me. You've heard me talk about this before and how I've attempted to add meditation into my life and I tried it before and I completely failed and bombed.[...]

"This experience intrigued me. I've heard interviews with other successful entrepreneurs, where meditation is mentioned. Tim Ferriss talks to a lot of people about their morning processes; Jaime Tardy from Eventual Millionaire also talks about morning rituals. There are many accounts describing what people do and give credit to in relation to their success, and meditation always comes up.

"At first I was like 'What is this woo woo thing? Is this some religious, spiritual thing?' I thought meditation was an inside joke, spread by those who 'meditated' to make others wonder about something that had no effect whatsoever but sounded like magic sauce...

"That's what I thought. I thought meditation was something 'weird.'"

I thought similarly, but urged on by Tony Stubblebine, I started meditating on a daily basis in July 2014. I had already been journaling consistently for a long while by that time. Many people have troubles starting meditation for the first time. They can't hush their own thoughts and focus on the practice. Thanks to my journaling habit, I had mastered this and found meditation easy.

Coach.me has millions of users, which means there's a lot of data to harvest. For example, in spite of what the majority think, the regular practice of meditation is only a bit more difficult than flossing your teeth.

Similar to journaling, the biggest advantages of meditation are awareness and increased focus. As Coach.me users revealed through a survey, it helps in many areas of your life.

Some examples:

-in relationships (respondents reported talking to their spouse without thinking about checking their phone messages)

-at work (respondents reported staying calm when a customer screamed at them, by practicing their breathing techniques)

Pat Flynn described the results he got from meditation in these words:

*"The big question is, is this actually having **any impact on my life**? Or is this just a weird way to spend time? Yes! I am seeing positive results from it. When I'm working I can actually catch myself getting off-thought and get back on track faster, and I feel a lot more focused during my work too, especially while writing."*

Notice that he wrote those words in January 2015 and he's consistently hit six-figure profits since that month.

Many successful people practice meditation: Clint Eastwood, Paul McCartney, Oprah Winfrey, Jane Fonda, Sting, Mick Jagger … Did you know that Kobe Bryant meditates to stay at the top of his game? That list of names should take care of one of the main obstacles to starting meditation: that it sounds woo woo and unappealing. What's the use of sitting and breathing? Well, Eastwood and Sting get something out of it, and others who do this believe they get tangible results. What else do you need to become convinced?

The second main obstacle for starting a habit of meditation is that for many it's just another thing they don't have time to do.

"You should sit in meditation for twenty minutes every day—unless you're too busy. Then you should sit for an hour." — Zen proverb

The good news: meditation doesn't have to take a lot of time. In fact, survey data confirms that a smaller initial commitment can increase your chances of continuing a meditation activity in the long term. When you start meditation, it's not the quality, but rather the quantity of your sessions that make it a habit. It's enough to persevere with an ultra-short, two-minute practice for eleven days. If you do, your chances of success in keeping that habit rises to 90%.

You don't have time to waste. Spend it on something that provides results. Start meditating.

Might you prefer meditation over journaling or tracking? It may offer a shortcut. You can get benefits from meditation starting with just two minutes a day. Compare that to the time you'll need for journaling. The time investment in meditation is miniscule. You just sit quietly for two minutes and you'll get some insights into yourself immediately. Unlike journaling, it may affect your days positively from the moment you begin this practice.

However, keep in mind that practitioners usually enjoy meditation immensely. If you start, you might spend just as much time meditating as I do journaling!

Remember:

- Meditation has many benefits including increased focus, memory, and productivity.
- Two main obstacles in starting the meditation practice are:
- Unreasonable disquiet about this activity. (Many successful people attribute a lot of their successes to meditation; its effectiveness is confirmed by university research.)
- Lack of time. (You may start from two minutes and can practice almost in any circumstances.)

Action Items:

- Reserve a couple minutes of your time, preferably in solitude (not obligatory, but very helpful).
- Sit or lie and relax (not obligatory, but very helpful).
- Close your eyes (not obligatory, but very helpful).
- Breathe deeply for two minutes, focusing on the air coming in and out of your nostrils (you can also focus on any of your body parts or sense your body in general); when a thought crosses your mind, acknowledge it and get back to your point of focus.
- Congratulations. You've just meditated for the first time in your life; repeat this process ten days in a row and you will develop a stable meditation habit.

8. PRAYER PUTS THINGS IN PERSPECTIVE

"It is better to aim high and miss than to aim low and hit." — Les Brown

If you are a religious person, prayer may be another tool for self-analysis. Every self-analysis technique comes down to you taking the time to know yourself and being one-on-one with yourself. Prayer is an excellent opportunity for this.

However, that's a rather agnostic perspective.

I'm fascinated by saints. I consider them the most successful people of all ages. Many of them accomplished marvelous works in this life and "secured" themselves the life eternal. No billionaire can claim the same thing. The very rich have a lot of worldly wealth, but will they have anything beyond this life?

In the last couple of years, I have read about 100 works written by saints. For many of them, prayer was their sole method of self-analysis. Most of them prayed incessantly. So, it's not just an interesting tidbit or a paragraph to fill the space in this book. The saints are among the most successful of any who've ever lived. Why aim lower than they did?

In prayer, you are not alone. Prayer is dialog with your Creator. And guess who knows you best in the universe? He created you. His providence guides you through hardships and happy moments. He designed you and raised you. He knows everything about your "reins and heart." And He loves you dearly.

You can spill out your heart in front of Him and God won't be surprised or horrified by the ugliness of your deeds and thoughts. He is the only Person with whom you can be totally honest without a risk of any consequences. Whether or not you realize this, in His eyes, you are completely transparent; you can't hide anything from Him.

When you approach your prayer with that attitude, the level of insight into your soul may be much deeper than in journaling or meditation. We almost invariably want to look good in the eyes of others and ourselves. Thus, we are inclined to lie to ourselves or to come up with excuses, to justify our wrongdoing or non-doing. And you simply can't do that with God. Sincere prayer cuts through all this sugarcoating like the proverbial hot knife through butter.

The way you pray, and the things you pray for, give an insight into your true soul. Plus, with divine help, you can shed some light on even the most hidden parts of your heart.

The Bible says that we were created in His image (Gen 1:27) and, what is more, in the end we are going to be like Him: "What we shall be in the future has not yet been revealed" (1 Jn 3:2). It's not possible to aim higher than that.

I won't recommend specific prayers or even ways you could add prayer into your day. Just keep in mind that even if it's a highly spiritual activity, all your down-to-earth elements of habit creation are still applicable in this case.

Start small.

I did. Compared with others who pray incessantly, my commitment is a minor one. I pray about half an hour a day. But when I first converted from the half-paganism, half-atheism in which I had lived before, I didn't pray even five minutes a day. It's taken me eighteen years to reach my current level of intimacy with God. If you are not already deeply committed to a daily prayer, don't overdo it. Sustainability is absolutely the most important trait of any self-analysis activity you undertake (if your goal is to get ongoing benefit from it).

Don't try too hard at the beginning by reaching for the most beautiful, elaborate, and lofty prayers of your religion. They are lofty because the people who created them were many levels above you. You may find no sense or feeling in them if your relationship with God hasn't developed that far yet.

Another self-analyzing activity closely related to religion, and commonly used by saints, is examination of conscience. It's a prayerful self-reflection on your deeds, words, urges, and thoughts. I don't know about you, but while I sometimes manage to tame my tongue from lashing out, my thoughts often run unchecked.

I still savor feelings of superiority and hold grudges; there are plenty of poisonous thoughts about others zipping around in my mind. And thoughts count; thoughts have an effect. Thinking such thoughts about others affects your mood and your actions.

A daily examination of conscience includes the potential downside found in tracking statistics—that you will overfocus on your failings. There is a lot of truth in "seek and you will find." If you look for evil in yourself, you'll surely see it, sadly. And so, an examination of conscience is not for beginners. You need a hefty dose of determination to examine your dark side day after day and not doubt yourself. But if you decide on this activity, keep in mind its goal. You're aiming to improve not to dislike yourself. Awareness is the first step to bettering yourself.

In a way, it's similar to what Benjamin Franklin did when he decided to develop himself. He didn't just pursue the traits he would like to possess. He examined himself, targeted the problematic areas, and then worked regularly on improving them.

Remember:

- What you pray for gives insight into your soul; you also invoke divine help, which vastly outperforms your conscious abilities.
- Saints' prayers are for saints.
- Examination of conscience is a prayerful self-reflection on your deeds, words, urges, and thoughts; this is an advanced technique for those who can face their internal ugliness without discouragement.

Action Items:

- Develop your own prayer habit; commit to a daily prayer.
- Select your own frequency, length, and type of prayer according to your current level of spiritual development.

9. YOUR MISSION

A personal mission statement *"focuses on what you want to be (character) and to do (contributions and achievements) and on the values or principles upon which being and doing are based."*[1]

Your mission is your personal constitution.

The process of creating your mission statement is a huge self-analysis task in itself. To define your own mission, you must simply know yourself. In his book, Mr. Covey provided some insightful questions and some even more useful imagination exercises. Do them, and you'll have a lot of information about yourself, your dreams, your fears, and intentions.

If you are task oriented and the idea of journaling for the rest of your life just doesn't feel right for you, the process of creating your personal mission statement may be a good introduction to a daily self-analysis discipline. As a goal-oriented person, your task will be clearly defined and the process of composing your mission statement should keep you occupied for at least a few weeks.

Once you have it, why not put it into use? A personal mission statement really works. For me, it works like a charm: it materialized statements I could barely embrace with my imagination. When I was creating my mission statement two-and-a-half years ago, I wrote, "I'm becoming a writer." Just one year later, I was able to refine it into "I'm a writer." If you had asked me a couple of years ago which of a few dozen sentences in my mission statement was the least likely to come true, that would have been my first choice.

I said that mission statements work "like a charm" because I have only a vague idea how they work. The results are indisputable, but the process itself seems like magic. Stephen R. Covey sold millions of copies of *The 7 Habits of Highly Effective People*, in which he explained the need for a personal mission statement and how it works. This book is highly esteemed in personal development circles and—more important—is recommended by its readers. If you need further validation of the mission statement concept, I recommend reading at

---

1. Stephen R. Covey, *The 7 Habits of Highly Effective People*

least the first two parts of Covey's book.

The exact mechanism is not essential, as long as it provides results. I just repeat my personal mission statement at least once a day.

My understanding is that my personal mission statement affects my life by channeling my attention to things I included in it. It can be explained best by a simple mind exercise. Put down the book for a moment and make a very brief scan of your surroundings. Look for things that are green. Try to find at least three items that are green. Start!

OK, you've scanned your environment looking for green. Without taking your eyes from the text, try to recall at least three items in your surroundings that are brown in color. Unless you are in an overwhelmingly brown space, you won't find that so easy.

When you give your brain a mission, it filters out any other inputs and focuses solely on the mission. You simultaneously stop being distracted by an overabundance of stimuli; you target your attention on just the few things that are helpful in fulfilling your task.

All you need to do to put your personal mission statement into use is to refer to it on a consistent basis. Feed your mind with your mission; your mind will do the rest on its own. I want to be an author who influences vast numbers of readers and affects their lives on a deep level. Now that my brain knows this, my internal guiding mechanism seeks opportunities to do just that. It pulls me away from activities that don't contribute to this mission, like reading news on the Internet. It facilitates any big decisions I must make, such as signing a publishing contract.

You can use your mission statement in several different ways. Stephen Covey recommended reading it at least once a day. That takes me a while. I wrote my mission statement with gusto, and it takes five minutes to read. Therefore, over time, I've come up with quicker and less time-absorbing methods: I recorded it and I can listen to it on my mobile whenever and wherever I want; I created a vision board related to it, and I can skim through that in less than a minute. And I repeat it in my mind at least once a day while my mind is not occupied: while walking, commuting, or doing the chores.

You can't create a mission statement without a hefty dose of insight into your soul. And the process itself teaches you useful techniques. I attribute to this process a lot of my self-analysis skills. As you know, I used to be a self-analysis nonentity. My negligence of this area might be described as legendary. Apart from a shy attempt at journaling, my creation of a personal mission statement was my first self-analysis activity.

What's in your mind determines your reactions and actions. Maxwell Maltz recommends you use imagination exercises as a remedy for every obstacle in your life. Of course, you can't force a circumstance to disappear from your life using your mind's power, but you can *always* use that power to affect your reactions to these unfortunate circumstances.

I learned to use visualization. I had poor results from trying to visualize because the images my mind delivers to me are not vivid. I need to put in a lot of effort to enliven these images with color, movement, and emotions. This was partly due to neglect. If you don't use something, it regresses. Imagination is no different. Prior to writing my mission statement, I'd never used my imagination to get to know myself. However, I am stubborn! I did the exercises recommended. I started to train my imagination, and I made visualization a part of my self-analysis arsenal.

Everyday use of your mission statement not only teaches you self-analysis, but it serves as the accelerator for your virtues and the jammer for your vices.

I've completely given up on negative conditioning.

In *The 7 Habits*, Mr. Covey advises using positive statements only if you want to improve your life. I'd advise it too, after my experiences using my mission statement.

In the original version of my mission statement, I'd included several negative statements at the beginning: *I don't do this; I don't do that.* But I've noticed that those negatively worded phrases were not especially effective in introducing the changes I desired. So I took out all the "don't" statements. I modified them to be positive statements. I replaced *I don't play computer games and mindlessly browse the Internet*, with *Every day I do everything in my power to fulfill my purpose.*

Today, I fight against my vices in the same way. I don't tackle them directly. Instead, I overload myself with positives, focusing on useful tasks that contribute to my well-being.

I deflect my vices by ignoring them. And each time I catch myself in a time-wasting activity, like compulsive e-mail checking, I don't beat myself up about it, but I immediately correct my course. Each of my noticed come-downs ignites me to take care of one of my disciplines, which brings me closer to fulfillment.

Constant attention and repetition of your mission statement, focused on the positives, activates the positive feedback loop. One of the areas I decided to work on when I created my statement, was parenting. As a concrete expression of my bond with my kids, I highlighted hugging as a way to develop and sustain our relationships. I don't know if we hug each other more than in the past, but certainly, I am more aware of it. I became a hugging machine. For example, yesterday my eleven-year-old son came to my home office while I was working and hugged me. I immediately noticed it on a conscious level, and I was present in the moment. I hugged him back; I gave him not only the warmth of my body, but also my attention.

Remember:

- A personal mission statement is your own constitution.
- Its creation is a huge self-analysis task, ideally suited to goal-oriented personalities.
- When you follow your personal mission statement, it will serve as the accelerator for your virtues, and the jammer for your vices.
- Daily usage of your mission statement ignites the positive feedback loop in your brain.

Action Items:

- Read the first two chapters of The 7 Habits of Highly Effective People and create your mission statement OR
- Read my blog post and follow my guidance: http://www.expandbeyondyourself.com/how-to-write-personal-mission-statement/

10. IN SUMMARY

"Wherever you are, just be there." — Jim Rohn

Let's recap the message of this book to solidify it in your mind.

Self-analysis is one of the foundations of success. Many successful people practice it, and sometimes it can be demonstrated that success has been a result of self-analysis. Marcus Aurelius' journal is such a case. The man was a ruler of the world in disturbing times. And it's hard to believe while reading his *Meditations*, but he was actually a great commander who won the wars he waged. Granted, circumstances were in his favor; he was practically born into the imperial family. He stayed in power not by luck or support of powerful friends, but by the virtues he mastered through constant self-analysis.

You are your most precious asset. Sometimes you are the only asset you have. I remember getting my first job in the IT industry back in the early 2000s. I had minimal experience. I had minimal skills. They weren't enough for the job I was given. I know that for sure because when I got it I needed to learn almost everything from scratch. I had absolutely no connections or support. And the unemployment rate in Poland was about 20% back then. I was hired because **I looked** like a guy who could manage to learn the rest.

In 2013, I started a writing career from scratch. Up to that point, I had published a couple of works: my master's thesis, which probably wasn't read by more than a handful of people other than the university staff who had to skim through it and award my degree; and a fantasy short story published online, read by several people and trashed in the comments. Not a promising beginning. But beginnings are only endings if you stop there.

To make it even harder for myself, I decided to publish in English, which is not my first language. I'm pretty much self-taught. Again, I had rudimentary skills: I knew some English, and I knew how to type, but that was about it. Not many resources for starting a new, highly competitive career. If you believe the statistics, digital publishing is one of the most competitive ventures in the world.

Objectively, my chances for success were about slim to none.

However, after eight months, I stormed the ranks of the best-earning authors in the world. At least 255,000 people had published something on Amazon before me. (I know, because it was my lowest author's rank ever) and I'm now ranked between 30,000 and 1,000. (It fluctuates day-to-day and depends on when my last promotion happened, and such things.)

The cause of this fabulous result has been largely my self-analysis; essentially, my growing self-development skills. Coincidently (if you believe in coincidences), I started my daily journaling sessions the same month I published my first book.

You are your only asset. Know yourself and you will overcome obstacles. Ignore your self-knowledge, and you're wasting vast resources you already have within you. In the end, it's not the *amount* of resources you have, either, but how you utilize them that will decide your success.

Having insight into your heart and mind will help you with everything. You create your wealth, health, relationships, career, and everything else in your life. Self-knowledge is your raw material; you can use it in any area of your life. Self-knowledge isn't like business knowledge— useful for entrepreneurship or career, but not very useful in other areas. Self-knowledge is applicable wherever you are, because you are there.

I started *Six Simple Steps to Success* series from this book, because I found my own self-knowledge so useful. Self-knowledge and the methods to gain it are universal. No matter your religion or skin color, where you live, what you do, how grim your past, or what you want to do *now* with your life, you can master it and use it to your advantage. It's a great starting point if you want to turn your life around or just correct your course.

This book is not a textbook.

I'm no expert in meditation, prayer, or journaling. I'm probably more skilled than the majority of the population in those areas, but there are still many better than I who already do a great job explaining these concepts and teaching in detail how to perform and excel with them. Even in the areas I am commended as knowledgeable, such as in crafting personal mission statements, I haven't provided detailed instructions.

Why?

Because my aim is not to have you blindly follow a set of instructions. I want you to seek the answers from inside yourself, or consult those with deep wisdom and mastery of the various techniques. You should always seek to learn from mentors who are suitable for you.

You'll find a whole journaling category in Self-Help on Amazon. And you'll easily find coaches who will teach you meditation. I assure you, however, that **you need very little in the way of outside help**. If I could start from scratch and reach as far as I have, you can feel confident in starting too, even with just the basic guidance I provided here.

Nonetheless, you may be determined to study some of the self-analyzing activities further, so I've listed, in the bonus section a few free resources.

But remember, knowledge alone counts for nothing; implementation alone holds the secret to success.

Remember:

- You are your most precious asset.
- Ignore your self-knowledge, and you're wasting vast resources you already have within you.
- Having insight into your heart and mind will help you with everything.
- Don't blindly follow a set of instructions when getting to know yourself.

11. LOOK IN THE MIRROR AND START NOW

You can start self-analysis today. It's not quantum physics or rocket science. It's a common human skill like speech, sensing the body impulses, or using one's imagination. In the most basic form, it just comes down to asking and answering questions directed at yourself.

You could begin, as I did, by jotting down your answers to this question: "What am I grateful for today?"

Even if you suck at it right now, you can always learn and excel at it. You can always find someone who is more advanced than you in any chosen field and use his experience to improve.

Often the reason you don't excel at something is that you don't consider it important. You don't pay enough attention to the activity, so naturally the level of your skill is low in that area. The main goal of this book was to reveal the importance of self-knowledge. I hope I drove the point home and you are ready to get to know yourself.

The exact method you choose to achieve that goal is up to you. I showed you the range of options. Choose the ones appropriate for you. If you are a hardcore atheist, I'm sure you won't start with prayer! If you have a vivid imagination, don't try to glue yourself to a journal for an hour a day. You know yourself best and what works best for you.

Here is your first self-analyzing exercise.

Ask yourself: Which method/s of self-analysis can I best sustain and develop into something bigger? Then start right now, right there. Transform your motivation into habit. Design your daily self-analysis disciplines and perform them day by day with stubbornness and persistence.

Once you design your self-analysis routines and practice them, they will redesign you. One thing leads to another. It's impossible to continue self-analysis exercises day by day, to know yourself more and more, and not develop yourself. It's like with physical exercise. If you show up every day at the gym and lift weights, your muscles just have to grow.

I started with a single simple discipline of writing one to three things I was grateful for about my wife. Nowadays I'm a gratitude fountain. I write 25+ gratitude entries in my three different gratitude journals. I also notice a lot of emotions, things, and events I'm grateful for during the day and acknowledge them in my mind. But it took me months to reach this level of satisfaction and happiness that I draw from my gratitude-related attitude.

I'm also fresh out of another yearly retreat with my church community. As usual, we were given a questionnaire with some life-and-death, vices-and-virtues questions. With the level of insight I'd gained through my own self-analysis, I was able to answer them swiftly, with a clarity I had not experienced before.

I've also noticed—and I think is more significant—that the same clarity and swiftness materializes when I tackle my everyday dilemmas: What is my priority right now? What should I do next? Where is it important to put my time and energy?

Each activity you design will change you and add to your development. Each new discipline in your routine will strengthen you.

As you know yourself better, you'll gain insight about your vices, and you'll realize what you should avoid or where you should focus attention to gain new positive traits. And each stage of this self-discovery process helps you to deepen your understanding and expand your mind.

I assure you; all you need is to begin and then to persevere. Even if you start with very small actions, just as I did, with one to three gratitude entries in my journal, and you apply patience and consistency, you may well finish with the self-knowledge of a sage.

Remember:

- In its most basic form, self-analysis is simply asking and answering questions.
- Self-analysis IS important.

Action Items (OBLIGATORY):

- Ask yourself: Which self-analysis methods suit me best?
- Start your first chosen method right now, wherever you are. Put down the book for a minute and jot down your thoughts, pray or visualize your life ten years from now.
- Design some relevant daily self-analysis disciplines, and perform them day by day with stubbornness and persistence.

BONUS: FREE RESOURCES

Here are some free resources to jump start your self-discovery journey:

There are a lot more, obviously. But if you spend all your free hours looking for the perfect self-analysis tools, you'll miss the point.

Effective self-analysis happens when you sit quietly and think.

1. DISC profile.

Here's the promotional description:

DiSC® is the leading personal assessment tool used by over 1 million people every year to improve work productivity, teamwork and communication.

DiSC® in plain language:

I took the test at the beginning of my transformation and repeated it a year later. The results helped me to know myself better at the very critical initial stage of my personal development journey.

You can take the full test for the price of your email address if you sign-up to Anthony Robbins' list:

https://www.tonyrobbins.com/ue/disc-profile.php

There is also a free sample available on the DiSC® creator's site. It will provide you at least some basic information:

http://discpersonalitytesting.com/free-disc-test/

2. The Most Important Questions to Ask Yourself

This is a short ebook written by my friend Lidiya. It includes several questions which can challenge your status quo if you answer them sincerely.

https://www.smashwords.com/books/view/432426

3. Blogs.

None of below blogs focus specifically on self-analysis, but each of them provides actionable and insightful information, something quite rare in the 'Internet fluff' era. These bloggers diligently study psychology, human behavior, the science of habits, and how the human brain works. They provide their analysis in easy digestible form.

I encourage you to use their experience instead of repeating their studies on your own.

http://jamesclear.com/blog
James writes mainly about habits and it's top-notch stuff.

http://www.startgainingmomentum.com/
Ludvig's blog is dedicated to young adults. He writes a lot about how human brain function. His articles about cultural trends are simply mind blowing.

http://www.basicgrowth.com/
Simon is a young Belgian and his blog is directed toward young men.

The main advantage of his blog is that Simon walks the talk. He writes about stuff he's experienced (and has analyzed why his results happened).

CONNECT WITH MICHAL

Thanks for reading all the way to the end. If you made it this far, you must have liked it! I really appreciate having people all over the world take interest in the thoughts, ideas, research, and words that I share in my books. I appreciate it so much that I invite you to visit my blog www.ExpandBeyondYourself.com.

Read a manifesto on my blog and if it clicks with you, there is a sign-up form at the bottom of the page, so we can stay connected.

Once again, that's

www.ExpandBeyondYourself.com

More Books by Michal Stawicki

You can find more books by Michal at:

http://www.ExpandBeyondYourself.com/about/my-books/

A Small Favor

I want to ask a favor of you. If you have found value in this book, please take a moment and share your opinion with the world. Just let me know what you learned and how it affected you in a positive way. Your reviews help me to positively change the lives of others. Thank you!

About the Author

I'm Michal Stawicki and I live in Poland, Europe. I've been married for over fifteen years and am the father of two boys and one girl. I work full time in the IT industry, and recently, I've become an author. My passions are transparency, integrity, and progress.

In August 2012, I read a book called *The Slight Edge* by Jeff Olson. It took me a whole month to start implementing ideas from this book. That led me to reading numerous other books on personal development, some effective, some not so much. I took a look at myself and decided this was one person who could surely use some development.

In November of 2012, I created my personal mission statement; I consider it the real starting point of my progress. Over several months' time, I applied numerous self-help concepts and started building inspiring results: I lost some weight, greatly increased my savings, built new skills, and got rid of bad habits while developing better ones.

I'm very pragmatic, a down-to-earth person. I favor utilitarian, bottom-line results over pure artistry. Despite the ridiculous language, however, I found there is value in the "hokey-pokey visualization" stuff and I now see it as my mission to share what I have learned.

My books are not abstract. I avoid going mystical as much as possible. I don't believe that pure theory is what we need in order to change our lives; the Internet age has proven this quite clearly. What you will find in my books are:

- Detailed techniques and methods describing how you can improve your skills and drive results in specific areas of your life

- Real life examples

- Personal stories

So, whether you are completely new to personal development or have been crazy about the Law of Attraction for years, if you are looking for concrete strategies, you will find them in my books. My writing shows that I am a relatable, ordinary guy and not some ivory tower guru.

Manufactured by Amazon.ca
Bolton, ON

11695002R00035